# CREATIVE ALCHEMY
12 steps from inspiration to finished novel

Creative Alchemy – 12 steps from inspiration to finished novel
©Sue Johnson

ISBN: 978-1-908342-00-3

Published in 2011 by HotHive Books, Evesham, UK.
www.thehothive.com

A CIP record of this book is available from the British Library.

Printed in the UK by TJ International, Padstow.

This book is dedicated to all my writing students –
past, present and future.

I wish you creative inspiration,
endless motivation and good luck.

*To Pauline*

*love & best wishes*

*Sue*
*x*

*Sue Johnson*
*28.10.2011*

According to the *Oxford English Dictionary*, the title of this book can be explained as follows:

*Creative* – inventive and imaginative

*Alchemy* – the medieval forerunner of chemistry – seeking to turn base metals into gold or silver

I see writing as a magical process that turns the base metal of your original idea into a memorable story. Turn the page – step into the magic...

# Contents

# Acknowledgements

I would like to acknowledge the encouragement I have received from my students at Number 8 Community Arts Centre, Pershore and at Farncombe Estate, Broadway and the enthusiastic way they have responded to the exercises I have set them – many of which are included in this book.

I would also like to thank my partner Bob Woodroofe for his love and support.

Special thanks also go to Karen Swinden, Sara Drinkwater, Charlotte McSwiney and the rest of the HotHive publishing team for their guidance and professionalism in making this book a reality.

# About the Author

Sue Johnson is a writer, artist and musician. She is published as a poet and is a member of Second Light Network. Her short stories have appeared in a variety of women's magazines – *Woman, My Weekly, Take a Break, Woman's Weekly, Chat, The People's Friend* and *That's Life – Australia*. Sue is a home study tutor for *Writers' News* magazine. Her first novel, *Fable's Fortune*, was published by Indigo Dreams Press in August 2011.

Sue has published her *Writer's Toolkit* series of booklets and CDs, designed to help writers at all levels. She runs writing workshops at Number 8 Community Arts Centre, Pershore, and for Farncombe Estate (www.FarncombeEstate.co.uk).

She enjoys organising and judging writing competitions, and giving talks to local groups.

# Foreword

By Sue Watson – author of *Fat Girls and Fairy Cakes* (published by Rickshaw)

My adventures in fiction began when I met writing teacher Sue Johnson. As a journalist and TV producer I was used to the written word, but had never considered a career writing fiction. I decided to enrol on a short course of creative writing and found Sue's 'can do' approach to all forms of writing really refreshing. Sue's classes encompassed all aspects and formats of fiction, which gave me the insights and tools to discover which one(s) suited me.

One of the hardest things for a new writer is to find a voice, but, encouraged by Sue, whose advice was to write 1,000 words a day (even if it's rubbish!), I began to hear a voice emerging in my work. Enlightened and excited by Sue's teaching, I began to write a novel. I wasn't always sure which direction I was going in, but Sue saw promise and urged me to continue, offering ideas and solutions to character and structural problems I often encountered.

One of the exercises Sue gave us in class was to present us with a box of random words written on pieces of paper. The word I picked was 'fairycakes' – which helped me to develop an idea for the book I was writing, which became *Fat Girls and Fairycakes*.

I may have started my novel without Sue – but like so many wannabe writers I would never have finished it, because I needed an experienced hand to hold. Sue offers that guiding hand to anyone who's thinking about writing a novel, or someone who's started a million novels and never finished them.

I can't recommend this book strongly enough – the writing exercises and advice alone will help you through the endless, tortuous, wonderful process of writing your novel. Then it will stay with you to the very last sentence – just before you write 'The End', and pop open the champagne.

# Introduction

I have always imagined the space inside my head as a pathway through a magic forest where stories live. Amongst the roots of trees are doorways that lead to other worlds beyond the one we are in. You can walk through a doorway and be whoever you like and wherever you like at any time in history – past, present or future. It's a bit like those dressing-up games you played when you were a child, when anything was possible.

Creating a story is a bit like becoming a child again and being able to play with the ideas that bubble to the surface. Many people complain that they don't have an imagination or that it has gone away. Rest assured – it hasn't.

We are all born with a lively imagination, but if it is not used it becomes like a rusty tap. As you start to build writing into your daily life, you will notice that you will begin to see things differently. In a short space of time the water of creativity will be flowing freely.

*Creative Alchemy – 12 Steps from inspiration to finished novel* aims to help you:

* maintain momentum and inspiration, and finish what you have started;
* write the best novel you can;
* improve your chances of finding a publisher.

Many people start novels and fail to complete them. The main reasons for this are:

* they don't prepare the ground properly first. Writing a book is a bit like planting a garden – you are more likely to be successful if the earth is weeded and raked before you plant the seeds;
* they don't think like a writer or commit regular time to their novel. Writing a novel takes a lot of energy and stamina;

★ what goes onto the page initially doesn't match what is inside their head, and they get discouraged – not realising that this is a normal feeling for most professional writers.

This book aims to help you clear any obstacles before you start, so that you can become the writer you were always meant to be – and keep going until you achieve your writing ambitions.

The five main reasons for a manuscript being rejected are:

★ not enough conflict (action);
★ characters weak or not believable;
★ dialogue weak;
★ settings not convincing;
★ not enough use of the senses.

The ideas and exercises in this book aim to help you address these points and write the best novel possible.

# Step One

Clear the Past

**Answer the following questions:**
1.   **Why do you want to write a novel?**
2.   **When would you like to complete it?**
3.   **How will your life change when you succeed?**
4.   **How will your book change the world?**

### Why do you want to write a novel?

If your answer to this is 'to get rich quick' – then think again. Some writers are true overnight successes. For a great many more, it can take ten years or longer to achieve this.

The best answer to this question is that you've got an idea that you're burning to get down on paper with characters that wake you up in the night with their clamour for you to write their story. You won't be happy until you have written the story.

### When would you like to complete it?

Most people work best if they have a deadline to work towards. Students have come to me with novels they have been struggling with for years and have not finished. Setting goals for each stage of the writing process helps to keep you focused on the task. It is better to allow yourself more time than you think you will actually need. Then you will be able to reward yourself for finishing early.

### How will your life change when you succeed?

Note that I have said 'when' and not 'if'! It might be something as simple as making you feel more confident, or proving to a sceptical partner that it's not going to be like the sweater or patchwork quilt you started making and failed to finish. Whatever your reason is, this may be what keeps you on track when things get difficult.

### How will your book change the world?

Think about the difference your novel could make. For instance, if it has a theme of a woman rebuilding her life after divorce, are there organisations that could benefit from the publication and sale of your book? Could you plan a series of talks or workshops to promote it and help other people at the same time?

**Are you wondering where to start?**
If you have never written before, then it is important to get into good habits from the start. Before you begin your novel, take a few weeks to establish a regular writing session. Think of this as being like training for a race. You wouldn't attempt to run the London Marathon without doing some training, would you? Writing a novel requires strength and stamina, so it is important to start exercising your writing muscle.

Buy the most attractive notebook you can find – and a pen that makes you feel like a writer. (It doesn't have to be expensive!) Aim to put something in your notebook every day – even if it is only one sentence. That is still one sentence more than you've written the day before.

Begin by listing three things you feel passionate about. If you haven't yet decided on a theme for your novel, the subject matter or some aspect of the main character could well come from one of these passions. For instance, mine would include Italian cookery, yoga and mother-daughter relationships. If you're stuck for inspiration, try the following:

★ problem-page letters
★ newspaper articles
★ poems
★ song lyrics
★ paintings
★ an item of clothing you once owned
★ proverbs

Many novels develop from a question posed by the author – for instance, Susan Page's *If I'm So Wonderful, Why Am I Still Single?* She wrote the book that attempted to answer this question, and met and married the man of her dreams before it was published.

Make a list of all the jobs you have had – including Saturday jobs, temporary and voluntary ones. Keep this list in your notebook. If you include some of these in your novels and stories it adds a grain of truth to your work – and something that publishers and agents call 'added value'. This means that readers learn something extra in the process of reading your novel or story.

The stories and poems that I have had published have all had an element of me in them – it might only be a very brief strand, but it is there nevertheless.

Remember that the characters in your story need passions of their own. It makes for an interesting story if these passions are in conflict with each other. Think about a female sheep farmer and a male property developer – or the other way round. Keep a list of any unusual jobs that you hear about, and check out any websites – for instance, poker-playing (www.professional-poker.com) and knife-throwing (www.knifethrowing.info/links.html).

If you belong to a national society or club that supports one of your interests – for example, dog breeding – then this could help to promote sales of your book when it is published.

### Looking after yourself

Writing is hard work – physically and mentally. It is also the most wonderful activity in the world, when things are going well.

Looking after yourself means that you make the most of your writing time, stay healthy, and enjoy life to the full.

- ★ Eat regularly. Don't be tempted to replace meals with biscuits and crisps. Have plenty of fruit and vegetables.
- ★ Drink lots of water.
- ★ Get as much sleep as you need! Many writers – me included – find themselves awake and writing during the night. Make sure you compensate for this at some stage, maybe by getting a few extra hours' sleep at the weekend.

* Learn to meditate.
* Practise visualisation techniques – both for your novel, and for your life as a best-selling novelist.
* Get up from your desk and do some stretches at least once an hour. (If you drink plenty of water, you'll probably need to move anyway!)
* If working on the computer, make sure you rest your eyes regularly. Take a few minutes to gaze out of the window or do some eye exercises. I find the ones below very helpful.
* Go for a brisk walk every day. It's good for your circulation – and you may also pick up some writing ideas.
* Join a yoga or tai chi class.
* Don't let writing problems get you down. Phone or e-mail a friend.
* Writing can be a lonely business. Build a support network.

### Eye exercises

Do this sequence of exercises three times a day.

### ➤ Exercise 1

Sit comfortably in a chair. Relax your shoulders. If you wear glasses, take them off. Without moving your head – just moving your eyes:

* look up towards the ceiling;
* look down towards the floor;
* look left as far as you can;
* look right as far as you can.

Do this three times. Then rub your hands together until they feel warm. Place them over your closed eyes for a count of twenty.

### ➤➤ Exercise 2

Again, without moving your head, imagine the wall opposite you has a giant clock on it. Follow the numbers round the clock face three times in each direction. As before, rub your hands together and place them over your closed eyes for a count of twenty.

**>>>    Exercise 3**

Make fists of your hands, leaving your thumbs upright. Place one hand at eye level close to you and the other at arm's length. Focus your gaze first on one thumb and then the other. Repeat this three times.

On completion of all three exercises, rub your hands together until warm and place them over your closed eyes for two minutes.

Three things to keep asking yourself as you write…

### What if…   Just suppose…   I wonder…

★    Stay curious and be prepared to experiment with ideas and structure. Don't expect to get things right first time. Keep trying.
★    Be bold. Take risks with your writing.
★    Just because something hasn't been done before doesn't mean it can't be done.
★    Ignore negative criticism and those people who expect you to have completed a best-seller in less time than they play a round of golf. Family and friends can often be your worst critics. Often this is because they are unnerved by the change in you.
★    Don't show your work to anyone until you feel ready to do so. Start slowly, build up gradually and keep going.

Begin by clearing your blockages

Negative criticism from the past still has the power to cause damage, and could prevent you from achieving your goal.

If this has held you back with previous projects, spend a few minutes thinking about who those voices are. Likely candidates could be your mother, an older sister who was always prettier or cleverer, or a teacher you never got on with at school. My inner critic sounds very like my old English teacher!

It is very important to get these voices working with you and not against you. It is said that you have about twenty seconds to replace a negative comment with a positive one, so have a reply ready. For instance, if the voice says, 'Huh, you think you can write a novel, do you? You're the one who never finishes anything'. Be ready with: 'This time it will be different.'

Call up your creative muse whenever you sit down to write. Invent a name, style of dress, favourite colour and fragrance for him/her.

Mine is called Anjali, and she smells of rose oil. She wears deep pink velvet embroidered with gold thread and she has thick dark hair in a single plait down her back, and violet-blue eyes. She can be relied on for a regular supply of creative ideas and she encourages the child-like creative side of me that loves fairytales. Take some time to think of a persona for your creative muse and keep something on your desk or writing space that reminds you of him/her. This could be a crystal or ornament, or a pendant or scarf that you wear when you are writing.

What does your critic look and smell like? Mine is called Mrs Majuba. She is a skinny old woman with grey hair scraped back in a bun. She has sharp elbows and knees, and wears plain black or grey skirts and jackets. She smells of TCP, and she thinks Anjali is totally frivolous and should be kept in check.

Imagine your muse and your critic having coffee together. What happens?

If you allowed either of them total freedom you would never complete your novel. If you are all creative ideas and no structure, you will never get anything written to a publishable standard. If you allow your critic to be too dominant, then your creative ideas will be suffocated at birth!

You need them both, but at different times. Creating and editing involve two different parts of the brain, so if you try to do both at the same time you will end up feeling frustrated and that you aren't getting anywhere. Your muse and your critic can't talk to you at the same time – they must take it in turns.

My solution was to construct a place for Mrs Majuba to stay until I am ready for her to cast her eagle eyes over my work. It's a black, wrought-iron gazebo with red velvet cushions (which she thinks are wildly extravagant, though she grudgingly admits that they are comfortable). She can sit there and read, or do her knitting, until I am ready for her.

Try doing the same with your critic. Tell them what you want from them – draw up a contract if it helps – and make sure they keep to it.

If you've cleared or noted any potential obstacles, then you are ready to begin.

---

**Magic Points**

★ List three things you feel passionate about.
★ List all the jobs you've had.
★ Think of questions to ask yourself or others – could they make a good story?
★ Who is your muse?
★ Who is your critic?

---

> **Exercise 1**

Pick an occupation from your list and write about someone doing that job. Pick another occupation that could potentially be in conflict with the first job – for example, café owner versus public health inspector. Write the beginning of the story.

>> **Exercise 2**

Write a scene where your muse and critic come face to face at the launch party for your novel. What do they say to each other?

>>> **Exercise 3**

What makes you feel angry, frustrated or sad? What would you be prepared to join a protest about? What led to this situation? Could this form part of your novel?

# Step Two

Are You Ready to Write?

'You're lucky to have the time' is the reaction I sometimes get when I tell people I'm a writer. The truth is that I don't have any more time than anyone else, but I create some for myself by getting up earlier, going to bed later, and not watching television.

Imagine you have a fairy godmother. Take a few minutes to write down three writing wishes.

Don't worry if they seem big or scary at the moment. You will grow into them!

These might be:

★ to finish a novel outline by Christmas;
★ to raise money for donkey rescue from sales of the book;
★ to go on television in order to promote the book and generate interest in (and funds for) a new donkey sanctuary.

Pin these wishes up where you can see them – or write them on the first page of your notebook. These will give you something to aim for – and a reason for writing the book.

Visualise an average day. Is there a small amount of time you could use to write? You can achieve a lot by using small pockets of time. Aim for fifteen minutes a day to begin with. It doesn't matter if you do this in three five-minute slots.

Keep paper and pens in the kitchen, sitting room, bathroom and car. I find ideas usually strike when I'm ironing, washing up or driving. It can be useful to have a Dictaphone in your pocket or handbag so that you can record ideas on the move (but not while driving!). I've also phoned home and left a much-needed line for a poem on my answerphone.

Carry your notebook wherever you go. Use it to jot down brief descriptions of people and places, and fragments of overheard conversation. You'll find these extremely useful for creating stories, poems and scenes in your novel.

Don't think you'll remember things when you get home. Ideas tend to evaporate like early morning mist if you don't pin them down.

My notebook often includes little sketches of scenes and objects, postcards and leaflets, leaves and flowers.

If possible, write at the same time of day. This helps to establish your writing as a habit. Plan your next session before you stop writing for the day – you are more likely to keep going if you can just continue smoothly rather than staring at a blank page.

Don't worry if what goes onto the page doesn't match the wonderful idea in your head. This is quite normal! Keep going. Write first drafts as quickly as you can – so that you get past your critic – if you haven't sorted somewhere for him/her to stay while you are working.

Most professional writers have a quota of words that they aim for every day. The average appears to be around 1,000 words a day. If you wrote 1,000 words a day for three months, that would give you 90,000 words – enough for a full-length novel.

Do what suits you best – whether that's maximising small pockets of time on a daily basis or doing a couple of longer writing sessions at the weekend. If possible, work at the time of day when your creative energy is strongest. If you are a lark it may suit you better to get up a few minutes earlier, whereas some people are at their most creative late at night.

Not all of us are lucky enough to have our own writing room or private space where work can be left out. Maeve Binchy used a tea trolley stored in the space under the stairs to keep her writing things on. You could use a box file or a plastic crate.

However, writing is as much about preparing the space inside your head – the pathway that leads to your story. It may help you to find a piece of music that symbolises the start of your writing time. Some writers begin by lighting a scented candle, whereas others may wear a particular garment or type of perfume, or place a crystal or special talisman in their work space.

If writer's block should strike, don't sit and stare at a blank screen or sheet of paper. It doesn't matter if you write badly – the important thing is to write. Pick a word, a book title or an item from a shopping list, and just start writing.

Reward yourself for the effort you put in. One writing friend of mine keeps a box full of small wrapped presents – chocolates, bubble bath, pretty pens – and treats herself to one when she feels she deserves it.

It is important to finish what you start, as this helps to build your confidence. If you are stuck for an idea for finishing a story, make a list of ten possible endings – it doesn't matter how silly some of them are, it's a good exercise in creative thinking. Choose the best one for that particular story. (Some of the other endings may encourage you to think of new beginnings.)

A publisher or agent will be interested in your previous writing experience. Start to compile a 'Writing CV'. Many people forget to mention writing they have done for work. Reports, letters, training programmes and articles for a company newsletter are all relevant experience.

Take every opportunity to get published – whether you are paid or not. Look at small press magazines to which you could submit stories, articles or poems. For example those published by Park Publications (www.parkpublications.co.uk) or The Yellow Room (www.theyellowroom-magazine.co.uk). Is there a local free newspaper that might be interested in a regular column? Buy a subscription to a magazine like *Writers' News* and check out any opportunities you find. Send for magazine guidelines, and follow the advice given. Competitions are good because they give you a deadline to work to, and some of them will give you a short critique which can be helpful in developing your work. Read the rules carefully before submitting your work.

Aim to have as many pieces of work as possible in circulation. You will then worry far less about rejection.

Keep good records of where, when and to whom you have submitted work.

Be patient. It can sometimes take up to six months before you get a response. Keep writing.

Look on rejection as part of your apprenticeship as a writer! Stay focused on your writing wishes. Allow yourself two days to grieve, and then move on. Read through your story again, reprint it, and send it back out as soon as possible. Remember that Tolkien was told *Lord of the Rings* was unpublishable, and that Joanne Harris's *Chocolat* was rejected 40 times before it was published.

Aim to re-use the same idea as many times as you can. For instance, a funny comment you overhear in a supermarket could begin as a letter to a magazine. This could then develop into a poem, a piece of flash fiction (also known as micro-fiction – usually less than 250 words), a short story, or song lyrics. Rewrite stories from different viewpoints. For instance, a love triangle could be written from the wife's, husband's or other person's viewpoint. If you change the settings and/or the time in history, then there is potential for even more stories.

Writing can be a lonely business. Take every opportunity you can to meet other writers. You may find a writers' circle helpful – but take time to find one that makes you feel encouraged and supported. If you don't find one that suits you, think about forming your own – or look for a 'writing buddy'. Go to writing workshops, poetry readings, talks and book signings.

---

**Magic Points**

★ Carry a notebook – and use it.
★ Write regularly.
★ Start thinking like a writer.
★ Finish what you start.
★ Recycle ideas.

---

### ➤ **Exercise One**

Make a list of three things you feel passionate about – for example, Italian food, motorbikes, old clocks. Write a short piece about one of them. Could you use this as the basis for a story or article? Can you think of a character who might be involved in this?

### ➤➤ **Exercise Two**

Go for a walk and jot down three things that you notice – for example, a pink umbrella, the smell of frying onions, or a red sports car being driven too fast. See if you can link these images in some way.

### ➤➤➤ **Exercise Three**

Go to a gallery and write the story behind one of the paintings – real or imaginary. Marina Fiorato wrote *The Botticelli Secret* – a fascinating novel inspired by a painting.

# Step Three

Developing Your Novel Idea

**This is my non-scary way of edging into writing a novel.**

Find a short space of time – half an hour is good – when you are not likely to be interrupted. (I have often parked the car in a quiet place to do this exercise.) Make yourself comfortable, and take off your shoes. Relax your shoulders, close your eyes and breathe deeply in and out four or five times.

Imagine you are watching the film version of your story. Visualise the scenes one by one and watch carefully. When you open your eyes, write down everything you can remember, paying particular attention to colours, smells and recurring images. You may need to repeat this exercise at regular intervals in order to get the full story or check certain details.

Who is the story about? What happened to them? Where is the story set? When? What is the incident or scene that the film begins with? How does the story end? What type of story is it (its genre) – for example, romance, sci-fi, fantasy, crime, historical?

Write down as many ideas as you can think of about the story on a large sheet of paper – wallpaper lining is good! Use different colour pens if this helps. Don't worry if some of the ideas contradict each other. Don't censor anything for the moment. Include descriptions, brief outlines of scenes and fragments of dialogue.

Take another large sheet of paper, some glue and a pile of old magazines (you can often find interesting ones in charity shops) and tear out any pictures, words or images that relate to the ideas you have. Create a series of collages. These can be pinned on the wall – or if wall space is limited, stuck on the inside of a wardrobe door so that you see them regularly. Some writers create a collage showing images of the life they will have when their novel is completed and published – the purple velvet dress they will wear to the launch party, the champagne, and the money they will be able to give to their favourite charity.

Your collages may give you more ideas about your novel and possibly inspire some scenes. Jot down any ideas that occur to you about characters, settings and storylines. Generate as many ideas as you can so that you have plenty of choice.

If you are able to go to the place where your novel is set, take plenty of photographs. Create a soundtrack. If it is safe to do so, sit with your eyes closed for a few minutes. What else do you notice? Does this give you any additional ideas?

Is there any basic research that you need to do to get started? Keep this to a minimum! There is a danger of getting so carried away with research that you never begin writing the novel. Start writing – you can fill in the gaps later.

You will create a lot of information that may not be used in the novel. Your story may not begin until your character is thirty, but certain events from their childhood may have an impact on the adult they have become, so it is important that you know what these are.

Choose a working title for your novel. It's a bit like giving a new baby a name. Take time at the editing stage to find the best possible title. This needs to be something that will attract the attention of a publisher or agent, so it should be memorable. There is no copyright on titles. I have had the most success with stories that have a colour or image in the title – for example, *The Blue Glass Jug, Red Ribbons, Cornflowers and Pink Meringues*.

Visit a large bookshop – preferably one where you can buy a cup of coffee. Spend some time looking at the sort of books you are interested in writing. Jot down any titles that appeal to you. Pick five of them and read the blurbs on the back covers.

What is it that would inspire you to open the book and begin reading the first chapter? Make a note of the information included in the blurbs and the type of words the writer has used.

Write down the working title for your book. Then write a back-cover blurb of approximately two hundred words.

When you are happy with your blurb, it is time to take things a stage further. (I call this my 'rolling stone' method of novel writing.)

Create a rough outline of the entire book. Treat this like an extended blurb. Aim for 2,000 words. It helps if you have an idea for the beginning and ending. Concentrate on the main plot line for now. Mention any possible subplots you may have thought of. The aim of this outline is to check that there is enough conflict (action) in the novel. (More about how conflict works later.) If there isn't enough action to engage the reader the publisher or agent will send your novel back very quickly. Look at places in your outline where you could add an additional plot twist. Reward yourself for the effort you have put in.

---

**Magic Points**

★ Create collages.
★ Don't get bogged down in research.
★ Jot down as many ideas as you can.
★ Find a working title.
★ Write the back-cover blurb.

---

➤ **Exercise One**
Go to a bookshop or library and jot down ten book titles. Choose these at random. See if you can use three of the titles as raw material to create a poem or piece of flash fiction.

➤➤ **Exercise Two**
Pick three elements from one of your collages and create a poem or part of a scene from your novel.

➤➤➤ **Exercise Three**
Imagine you are one of your characters. Begin with 'I remember' and write for ten minutes without stopping.

# Step Four

Plots and Subplots, Themes and Fairytales

The plot is the engine that drives the story forward. The main plot line should run from the beginning to the end of the story, and the idea should be big enough to sustain this.

A plot is a series of related ideas that make up the action of the story. It is thought that one reason why Jane Austen's novels are still so popular is that she has a plot twist every few pages – a new character, situation or complication that keeps the story fresh and interesting.

The ingredients of a plot are:

**Situation**
**Complication**
**Crisis**
**Resolution**

In a novel, there will be a number of complications – all designed to make things as difficult as possible for your characters – before the final resolution.

Before things are resolved, there is nearly always a 'black moment' when it appears that all is lost – before the final plot twist and the end of the story.

Make sure that you foreshadow events effectively. For instance, if your heroine once worked in a circus, then it would be acceptable that she is more confident than others in stopping a runaway horse.

If your hero is going to be abducted by the press gang, then make sure that some mysterious disappearances are mentioned earlier in the story, so that the reader's sense of expectation is aroused.

Flashbacks can help to add depth to characters and situations, but should be used sparingly. If you are tempted to keep going back in time, maybe the story needs to start at an earlier point in the character's life.

The ending doesn't necessarily have to be 'happy ever after', but it should suit the mood and atmosphere of the story. It is said that the first page will sell this novel to your reader, and the last page will sell them your next book.

Don't be tempted to rely too heavily on coincidence. Used sparingly, it can be effective. If overdone, you risk your reader saying 'As if!' and throwing the book aside.

Your reader needs to care enough about your characters and the situation they are in to keep turning the pages.

Subplots add depth to the main plot and give more information about characters and settings. These should complement the main plot, not try and take over from it. Don't make the mistake of including too many of these, or your story will become fragmented.

For instance, if your main plot features a kitchen maid called Emma who ends up marrying the squire's son, then you could have one subplot featuring the stable lad who had hoped to marry Emma, and the revenge he takes on the couple. Another subplot could feature Emma's younger sister Alice and her brave action that saves the couple's lives when she overcomes a serious problem of her own, outwits the stable lad and finds a love of her own.

All strands of the plot should be woven together like a plait by the end of the story.

Re-read three novels that you have particularly enjoyed – and make a careful note of the main plot points, how many subplots there are, and how the stories fit together. Are there any similarities in their structure? Could any of these ideas help with the plot and structure of your novel?

Most novels have a theme which can be summed up in a few words – for example:

★ rags to riches
★ cheats never prosper
★ love conquers all
★ good triumphs over evil
★ the underdog succeeds.

You may be asked by a publisher or agent to sum up your novel in a dozen words. If you begin by telling them it's a 'Cinderella story' or a 'good triumphs over evil story' they will have some idea of what to expect.

Read some women's magazine stories. See if you can spot the themes. Make a list of these in your notebook. Could you write some new stories using these themes as inspiration?

The plots of many modern novels and films are based on fairytale structures. These work because the rhythm of these stories is so ingrained in the mythology of every culture that we do not question it. Stories were the earliest counselling tools. Long ago, before stories were written down, if you had a problem you would visit the local healer or wise woman and be told a story which would, hopefully, help you to solve it.

Fairytales were not just meant for children! The original versions were a lot more graphic than the tidied-up versions presented by the Brothers Grimm.

With fairytales, there are two basic plots – either the hero goes on a journey, or someone new comes to town and upsets the situation.

Fairytales are about missing pieces. Many of them begin with the death of a parent or something else going drastically wrong in the main character's life. Numbers are significant in fairytales. Seven is the most widely used number in any culture. It occurs a huge number of times in the Bible and the Koran, as well as in book and film titles – for example, *Seven Brides for Seven Brothers*, *Seven Pillars of Wisdom*, *Seven Secrets of Happiness*.

Three is the next most widely used number – and the one that is possibly most useful to fiction writers.

### Imagine this

Imagine that a young woman called Caroline is walking home alone one dark night. She was hoping to get a lift home, but it didn't happen. She separated from a violent boyfriend a few weeks ago and is scared that he is going to attack her. The street she is walking down has alleyways at regular intervals between the houses – dark places where someone could hide. There is no moon, and a strong wind is blowing.

Something moves in the shadows at the edge of the path. Caroline jumps out of her skin, but it is only a large sheet of plastic blown down the alley by the wind.

She keeps walking, imagining she can hear footsteps behind her, reliving some past situations with her boyfriend.

Something else emerges from the shadows, making her jittery again. This time it's a black cat. Caroline pauses to stroke it, laughing at herself for being so nervous, especially as she's nearly home now.

She walks a few paces forward. Her boyfriend steps out in front of her, his menacing smile illuminated by the sodium orange streetlight.

Hopefully you can see from this brief example how raising the reader's expectations and then reducing the tension helps to keep the reader wondering what will happen next. If this was a scene in a novel, it wouldn't have nearly as much impact if the baddie just stepped straight out in front of Caroline when she left work.

It will add depth to your novel if you introduce conflict situations in threes.

Look at the number of myths and fairytales that have three in the title. There are three wise men in the Christmas story; in most fairytales events happen in threes, or when there is a choice to be made it is usually between three options – for example, three boxes or three wishes. Study the structure of fairytales and see how they could strengthen your novel.

You may have heard other writers talk about the 'mythic plot'. This is the basic structure for a number of modern commercial novels, Hollywood films – and the Harry Potter stories.

The twelve stages of the 'mythic plot' are:

1. **The hero in his usual environment.**
2. **The call to adventure.** (This could be a piece of information, a letter or an event indicating the start of a complication – or it could be a person.)
3. **Refuse the call.** (There is some reason why the character doesn't take up the challenge.)
4. **Encouraged by a mentor.** (For example, the wise woman in a fairytale.)
5. **Cross the first threshold.** (In a fairytale this may be going through a door or over a bridge. The hero has moved out of his comfort zone.)
6. **Meet friends and enemies.** (He's not sure who can be trusted.)
7. **Approach the innermost cave.** (This could be an aspect of himself he is trying to deal with – for example, an addiction of some kind.)
8. **Fight the monster.**
9. **Take the treasure.**
10. **The chase.** (The monster comes back to life.)
11. **The final battle.** (Where the monster gets hacked to bits.)
12. **Return to the ordinary world.** (The hero has changed because of the experiences he has had.)

**Magic Points**

★ Keep a list of possible themes in your notebook.
★ Sum up your novel in a few words.
★ Look at fairytale structures and see how they could work for you.
★ Look at the significance of numbers.
★ Focus on your ideas.

➤ **Exercise One**

Re-watch a favourite film and jot down some notes about the structure. Does it give you any ideas for your own work?

➤➤ **Exercise Two**

Make a list of fairytales in your notebook. Choose one of them and rewrite it in a modern setting. Play the 'what if?' game. For instance, what if the three bears were running a drugs den in the woods and Goldilocks was a young female detective...?

➤➤➤ **Exercise Three**

Jot down a list of themes in your notebook. Use these as warm-up exercises before you begin writing – or for those days when you feel uninspired.

# Step Five
## Developing Your Outline

*Who* is the story about? The main character will usually be the person with the most at stake.

*What* do they most want? This should be something really important – preferably with a difficult choice attached to it.

*Who/What* is preventing them from achieving this? What choices do they have?

You may find the 'conflict circle' on the next page helpful for developing this.

Imagine this

The story is set in 1920. Hannah Martin is 18 and lives in London. She has just lost her job as a housemaid because the wife is jealous of Hannah's beauty and the effect this has on her husband. Hannah needs money desperately because her younger sister, Amelia, who she adores, is ill and needs proper medical treatment. Hannah's money has been providing for Amelia.

Her options are:

★ get another job
★ accept an unwanted proposal of marriage
★ sell something of value
★ become a prostitute
★ go to a money lender
★ steal the money
★ ask her grandfather for help
★ set up a business of her own.

When you have decided what your character's problem is, write this in the square in the middle. Then write the options they have in the eight 'wedges'. For each option, think of at least one reason why they wouldn't do this.

## **Conflict Circle**

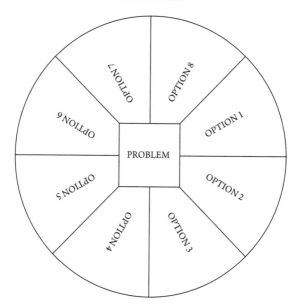

For instance:

★    Hannah's preferred option would be to get another job, but she has been dismissed without a reference.

★    Someone has proposed marriage, but she doesn't trust him.

★    The only thing of value that she has is her mother's locket, and she cannot bear to part with it.

★    She is determined not to become a prostitute because the lady who dismissed her told her that was where she would end up.

★    Her father was ruined by borrowing money.

★ She is too honest to steal anything.
★ Her parents quarrelled with her grandfather and were cut out of his will.
★ She has no money to set up any sort of business.

Whichever option you choose for your character, this should then spark a series of other problems.

For instance, Hannah could be lucky enough to find another job – but then comes into contact with the obnoxious lady who dismissed her and is still out to make trouble for her. She finds herself back to square one.

Go through the brief outline you have written and look at places where you could put in additional plot twists. Don't let your characters solve problems too easily. Give them difficult choices. Build the emotional tension.

Have an idea as to what your ending might be. It's a bit like having a finishing post to aim for at the end of a race.

Take a big sheet of paper and jot down as many situations and problems as you can for your character. Keep the main problem as the central focus – in Hannah's case, her much-loved sister's declining health and the urgent need for money to pay for medical care – and throw a whole series of spanners into the works.

The way I work is to then 'brainstorm' twenty key scenes, moving from the beginning to the end of the novel. (You will probably end up with more than this as the novel develops.)

Some writers work in pairs to do this – suggesting scenes to each other. It is certainly the way that most comedians work.

Keep visualising the scenes in your novel. With practise you will find you can do this in bank and supermarket queues, and during boring meetings.

Write each scene on a numbered postcard. If you keep these in an A5 plastic wallet (available from most supermarkets and stationery shops) you will then have a 'novel in miniature' in a format that makes it easy to carry with you anywhere, and to work on when you have a few spare minutes.

Aim to develop each postcard into a 2,000-word scene. By the time you have done this, your book will be at least 40,000 words long and you will be able to see where the gaps are and where more action is needed.

Keep a notebook specifically for your novel and jot down any ideas you have about characters, settings, scenes and subplots.

Create a spider diagram (see the next page for an example) or do another 'conflict circle' if you hit a blank wall and can't imagine what happens next.

Think ahead to what your chapter headings might be. Is there a recurring image or theme throughout the book that could act like a series of pegs to hang the story on? For instance, in Nigel Slater's autobiography *Toast*, all the chapter headings are an item of food. In *Daughters of the House* by Michele Roberts, they are items of furniture.

Try making a list of possible ideas that could link characters and situations and help the story to flow from beginning to end.

### If your ideas aren't flowing...

Sometimes inspiration is hard to find. Even if you have time, there may be a family crisis or some other problem that takes up your mental energy and pulls you away from your novel. It's at these times that it's easy to lose the thread and stop writing. The longer you've stopped, the harder it is to get going again. If this happens to you, try one of the following strategies and keep hold of that thread.

## **Spider Diagram**

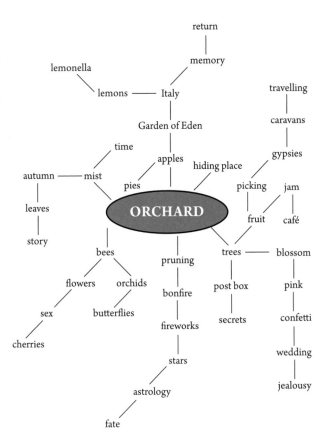

★ Make a soundtrack of your story. If it was a film, what would it sound like?

★ Soak in a bath with a glass of wine and think about one of your characters doing the same thing. What sort of bubble bath would they use?

★ Go shopping. Buy something your main character would like. Keep it on your desk for inspiration.

★ Sit in a café and do some people-watching. Can you find any new characters?

★ Work in the garden. Sow some seeds. Pull up weeds.

★ Ask 'what if?' questions about situations and characters.

★ List your main character's interests and find out about, or try, one of them – for example, Italian cookery, beekeeping, yoga.

★ Look at the clouds or the stars and imagine one of your characters doing the same thing. What do they see and feel?

★ Just start writing – don't worry about getting it right.

---

**Magic Points**

★ The idea needs to be 'big' enough to sustain the whole novel.

★ What does your main character most want?

★ What is stopping them from achieving this?

★ Create your own portable writing desk.

★ Write key scenes on index cards.

---

> **Exercise One**

Complete a 'conflict wheel' for your character. Fill in all the eight spaces. For each option, think of at least one reason why this course of action would not be appropriate. Does this give you more ideas for your novel?

>> **Exercise Two**

Using the above exercise, choose three of the options and write a series of scenes showing what could happen to your characters.

### ➤➤➤   Exercise Three

Think of the following:

★   A person's name
★   A place
★   A time of day
★   A time of year
★   An emotion they are feeling
★   Something they are carrying that they want to get rid of.

Write the first two paragraphs of a scene or story.

# Step Six

Your Characters

Start thinking more about your characters. You should aim to know them better than some of your own family!

Begin by looking for magazine pictures that remind you of them. If your novel became a film, who would you choose to play the various roles?

I have included at the end of this chapter the character questionnaire I use for my own novels. You may have additional questions that you'd like to ask them.

Bear in mind that a lot of this information may not be used in the novel, but it will add depth to characters and situations if you are aware of it. It's a bit like an iceberg. You may only use ten per cent of the information you have, but the structure of the novel is stronger because you know more.

If your characters have a past as well as a future, they will become more rounded. Take time to consider what has happened to them earlier on in life – possibly a long time before they stepped into the pages of your novel.

Names are important – and it may take time to find the right one. Begin writing anyway, and don't worry if you reach the end of the first draft and find that some of the names don't feel right. Jot down any alternative ideas in your notebook.

What was your character's childhood like? Does it provide reasons for the way they behave in later life? For instance, if a boy sees his father behave badly towards his mother, does it affect the way he treats women when he is older?

Don't make your characters too perfect or too evil. Give them flaws and redeeming features. A character who commits burglaries may well be doing so in order to fund his much-loved brother's hospital treatment.

A girl who is beautiful may have an impetuous streak that leads her into trouble.

A boy who isn't very clever may have a kind nature and, by missing an important interview to help somebody, could end up with a better job as a result of his actions.

Think about ways of *foreshadowing* future events in your novel.

Imagine this

Olga, a fit and sprightly 75-year-old, is waiting in the queue at the bank. Something on one of the posters reminds her of her teenage years when she ran away from home to join the circus. She met Dan, who became her husband, and they did a knife-throwing act together. He still jokes about how good her aim was.

Olga is lost in her world of memories, and doesn't at first notice the disturbance at the front of the queue. A man in a hoodie has pulled out a gun and is demanding money from the cashier.

Without a second thought, Olga pulls a potato out of her shopping basket and throws it at the man, hitting him on the arm so that he drops the gun. It clatters across the marble floor and a customer picks it up. The bank robber is overpowered, and a plump lady with blonde curls sits on him until the police arrive.

Look at how famous writers foreshadow events and raise the expectation that something is going to happen later in the story. In an early chapter of Charles Dickens' *Tale of Two Cities*, a cask of wine is dropped and the red wine flows down the cobbled streets of Montmartre, foreshadowing the blood that will flow later in the story at the height of the French Revolution.

Imagine you had to play your character in a film. How do they walk into a room? If they sit on a chair, are they sitting upright with their back straight, or do they kick off their shoes and flop into an armchair with their knees tucked up, hugging a cushion?

Don't forget to feed your characters! I have critiqued a great many novels where food is never mentioned. Food in a story can provide a huge range of colours, sounds, smells and textures. It can also be extremely sensuous.

How does your character eat? It has been said that this can mirror how they behave in the bedroom. If they gobble down a meal without really tasting it, then it's possible they may behave in the same manner between the sheets! (I haven't put this to the test – but it sounds plausible!)

Imagine one of your characters eating a chocolate éclair. Do they eat it with a cake fork so they don't get their hands covered in cream – or do they pick it up and take big bites, licking their fingers when they've finished and ending up with chocolate round their mouth? Or would they refuse to eat one at all? How do the other characters react to the way they eat – with amusement, or embarrassment?

What sort of kitchen does your character have? Is it one of those ice-white immaculate rooms that always smells of multi-surface cleaner, where nothing is ever cooked because the residents either eat out or have take-aways – or is it a cheerful family space full of children and dogs, with the cooker top crammed with bubbling pans of home-made vegetable soup and the windows steamy with condensation?

If they cook anything, do they follow a recipe exactly or do they throw everything into the pot, including a generous splash of red wine, and see what happens?

Is the floor sparkling clean with that just-mopped look – or is it patterned with animal paw-prints, and is there a cat blinking lazily by an open fire?

### Secret camera in the bedroom

Imagine you have a secret camera that can follow your characters to the bedroom. Watch them as they get undressed for bed. In what order do they take their clothes off? Does this change if they have a new love interest?

Where does your hero put his loose change? On the bedside table, wrapped in a tissue on the floor by the bed, or in his left shoe?

What sort of sheets (fabric and colour) does he have on the bed? How often are they washed? Is he used to 'entertaining' a variety of women here?

Does your heroine have a beauty routine at night – or does she flop into bed with her make-up still on? What sort of products does she use – designer label, or supermarket value range?

Is your character tidy or untidy? Does this cause a problem with anyone else? What would they most like to get rid of?

What sort of a lover are they? Are they a caring or a selfish partner?

What do they wear in bed?

What do they do if they can't sleep? Count sheep, read a book, watch telly? What happened when they were a child and couldn't sleep? Were they ignored, or did someone cuddle them and tell them stories?

What is the first thing they do when they get up in the morning? Do they have a bath or a shower – or do they dive out of bed at the last minute and never have time for a proper wash?

Do they put their clothes out the night before – or is it a frantic scramble through the wardrobe to find something that's not creased?

### Secret camera in the bathroom
Firstly, do they have a bathroom? If your novel is historical, your characters may be using a tin bath in front of the fire, or washing in the scullery where you'd find the only tap. They may have to share a privy with ten other families.

If they have a bathroom, what is it like? What sort of bathroom would they have if they could choose? Is it an en-suite, or do they have to share it with the rest of the family?

What colour is it? What can you smell? Are the towels thick, white and fluffy, or thin and worn and stained with old mascara?

What do they keep in their bathroom cabinet? Are they taking any medication? Do they wear glasses or contact lenses?

Do they use spray or roll-on deodorant? What brand of toothpaste do they use? Normal or electric toothbrush? Electric razor or wet shave (hopefully men only!)?

Hair dye? Nail varnish?

Do they take ages in the bathroom in the morning, raising the stress levels of everyone else in the house, or are they really quick? Do they leave the bathroom tidy, or is it a mess of wet towels on the floor and the bath not cleaned? Do they get dressed in the bathroom, or return to the bedroom?

What perfume or aftershave do they use? How do others feel about it?

What memories do they have of childhood bath-times – maybe sharing with a brother or sister? (Include some of your own memories here.)

Take time to visualise your characters in various personal situations. It will help to increase your knowledge of them. Be aware that you might be asked obscure questions by a publisher or agent. (I was once asked what brand of toothpaste my hero used, and where he put his loose change at bedtime.)

Write any key information about your characters on a postcard or index card. It is very easy for things like hair and eye colour to change during the process of writing the novel!

**Magic Points**

★ Create a family tree for your character.

★ Find out as much about them as possible.

★ Use any surplus information to create poems and short stories.

★ Give your reader a reason to care about them.

★ Create index cards so that their eye and hair colour doesn't change as you write the book. Add photos and magazine pictures.

➤ **Exercise 1**

Jot down three childhood memories you could use in your novel. Write up one of them in more detail. Include a colour, a time of year and an item of food.

➤➤ **Exercise 2**

Imagine your character getting dressed in the morning. Are they in a panic because they are running late, or have they laid their clothes out ready the night before?

Is this an ordinary day, or are they going somewhere special? Is it somewhere they are looking forward to going? What item of clothing do they put on first? How do they look when they are dressed?

➤➤➤ **Exercise 3**

Give your character a health check. What medical problems have they had in the past?

Write about a childhood illness that they had – or a time when they had to stay in hospital. What medical problems do they have now? Do they look after themselves, or do they neglect their health?

**Character questionnaire**
Think about the following:

| | |
|---|---|
| Name | |
| Birthday and star sign | |
| Parents | |
| Where was he/she born? | |
| Brothers and sisters | |
| Childhood | |
| Education | |
| Greatest fear | |
| Greatest secret | |
| Favourite toys/games/ colours/food | |
| Illnesses | |
| Day or night person? | |
| Interests | |
| Religious beliefs | |
| Dreams/ambitions | |
| Temperament | |
| List twelve key events in their life to date | |
| Relationships | |
| Favourite animal | |
| Favourite music | |
| Generous or mean? | |

A copy of the character questionnaire can be downloaded from
www.writers-toolkit.co.uk.

# Step Seven
Who is Speaking? Dialogue and Viewpoint

The function of dialogue in a story is to:

★ show the characters in action
★ give more information about the setting
★ give more information about the plot
★ increase dramatic tension.

It may sound obvious, but your characters should sound different from each other!

Visualise the film of your story again – with the sound turned up.

Tracy Chevalier imagines her characters as musical instruments. Vermeer in *Girl With A Pearl Earring* is a double bass made of rich dark wood, whereas his wife is something brassy and discordant.

If your characters speak in a particular dialect, it is better to give a flavour of this on the page, and then just refer to the character's 'soft Irish lilting voice', for example. Too many dropped aitches can look like a cluster of tadpoles moving across the page.

Try removing the speech tags from a section of dialogue, and put it away for a couple of weeks. Read it again. If it is not obvious who is speaking each line, then you need to do some more work.

Everyone has their own pattern of speech and favourite expressions. Make sure this is true of your characters too. There's a lovely character called Alicia in Robin Sisman's novel *Weekend in Paris*. She's Australian and pronounces her name 'Uh-lee-sha'. Her accent is described as 'ripe and rich as Camembert running off the plate'. She talks about needing a 'whiz' when she's heading towards the bathroom. Both details, together with her forthright stance, make her instantly recognisable.

Don't forget facial expressions. These are important, as sometimes what the characters say doesn't mirror what they are thinking. You can add some good plot twists in this way.

## Imagine this

John is having dinner with Sylvia – a woman he is pretending to be attracted to. Sylvia is a wealthy widow and John's real intention is to get his hands on some of her money and then murder her.

The courtship hasn't been easy – every time John thinks he's making progress, something happens to mess things up. Tonight, however, everything is going well. It's her birthday, they're enjoying a candlelit dinner, she's drunk more wine than is her usual habit, and she seems to John like a plum ripe for picking.

Sylvia gazed at him across the white tablecloth. 'Do you love me, John?'

'Of course I love you,' said John, thinking of the little place in Spain that would soon be his.

## Scene and summary

Many new writers shy away from writing dialogue, but it is an important part of most novels and short stories. If you are trying to reduce your word count for the novel then it's a good idea to read through what you have written and see if there are any scenes that could be cut and replaced with a brief summary of the action.

Similarly, if you are looking to increase your word count and build in more action, turning a brief summary into a longer scene could achieve this.

## Which has more impact?

Nick and Anna were at a party. They had an argument after she saw him talking to another girl. (Summary)

Nick confronted Anna in the garden. She was sitting in the shade of the laburnum tree sipping a glass of iced water, taking no part in the lively birthday party erupting around her. Her air of detachment irritated him.

'Why are you being such a misery tonight?'
'Have you ever thought it might be something to do with the way you behave?' Her voice was silky-smooth.
'What do you mean?'
'I mean that I'm sick of you ignoring me whenever we go out, and coming on to every other woman – like that blonde you were talking to earlier.'
'What's got into you tonight? You're not drinking, you're not dancing, you're not even trying to have a good time.'
'As I tried to tell you last week before you changed the subject and walked out, our relationship's been dead for a long time now. I want you out of my flat and out of my life. For your information, I'm not drinking because I'm pregnant – and it isn't yours.' (Scene)

Look at other ways of giving information, other than narrative and dialogue – for instance:

* ★ letters
* ★ telegrams (if historical fiction)
* ★ e-mails
* ★ text messages
* ★ newspaper articles
* ★ TV news reports
* ★ diaries
* ★ shopping lists/wish lists.

Adding variety will help to add texture to your writing.

Viewpoint

* ★ Who is telling the story?
* ★ Whose problems provide the storyline?

★ Who has the biggest emotional stake in the story?
★ Who is the most interesting character?

## First Person Singular Viewpoint
The advantage of this is that it's a very natural way of writing, with no need for 'thought tags'. The disadvantage is that you can only see things from that one perspective, so the novel or story needs to go more deeply into that person's psyche or have much more action in it.

## Third Person Singular Viewpoint
The story is told from the viewpoint of one of the characters, but they are referred to as 'he' or 'she'. This allows the reader to become the character and is the viewpoint to go for if you want maximum reader involvement.

## Second Person Single Viewpoint
This is very difficult to maintain for a whole novel. The best example of this is *Bright Lights, Big City* by Jay McInerney.

## Third Person Multiple Viewpoint
You can write from the hero's viewpoint in one chapter and the heroine's in the next. The advantages are that it adds tension and gives all sides of the story. On the other hand, if you have too many changes of viewpoint, the story can become fragmented or confusing.

---

### Magic Points

★ Dialogue should tell us more about the characters and move the story on.
★ Stick to 'he said', 'she said'.
★ Language used should suit the characters concerned (use a dictionary of slang if necessary).
★ Show the characters in action as they are speaking.
★ Do their words mirror their thoughts?

➤ **Exercise 1**

Choose one of the following summaries and write it into a full scene.

Daisy and Ruby were having tea in the garden. They had an argument about the bracelet Ruby was wearing.

Jane and Tom argued on the eve of their wedding. He stormed off.

Grace and her mother had lunch together. As usual, her mother kept going on about wanting to be a grandmother. Grace got upset and walked out.

Could you develop one of these ideas into a short story?

➤➤ **Exercise 2**

One of your characters is feeling irate about something. Write a monologue for them detailing what happened and how they reacted.

➤➤➤ **Exercise 3**

Choose two characters who are at a wedding and have a completely different attitude to what is going on, and write ten lines of dialogue without using any 'he saids', or 'she saids'. Is it easy to tell who is speaking when you read it out?

# Step Eight
Conflict, Pace and Tension

Conflict means action. There needs to be enough action in the story to keep the reader interested so that they keep turning the pages to find out what happens next. If your reader doesn't care about what happens to your characters, they will soon put the book down and find something else to do.

Conflict in a story should be on three levels:

★ A character's battle with some aspect of themselves – for example, an addiction to alcohol or gambling, an eating disorder, a low level of self-esteem, or agoraphobia.
★ A character's battle with someone else – a woman who wants to leave her controlling boyfriend, a girl who can never please her mother, or a man who has an overbearing boss who is causing him problems.
★ A character's battle with some aspect of their environment – getting caught in a thunderstorm and missing the last bus home, getting stranded on a beach with the tide coming in, or a car breaking down.

Aim to have a balance of conflicts in your story so that there is always a new plot twist. Don't introduce just one problem at a time – send them in threes. Play the 'what if?' game with this, to keep things interesting. Look at how putting a time limit on a situation raises the tension (for example in James Bond films). Write down as many environmental factors as you can that could influence your story.

### Imagine this

What if a woman called Hazel suffers from agoraphobia (**Conflict situation 1**)? She has a daughter called Sally. Her daughter's neighbour rings to say she urgently needs her help. Sally has gone into labour with her second child, things aren't going too well at the hospital, and two-year-old Jessica is inconsolable and asking for her granny. Please can Hazel come at once? (She is unaware of Hazel's agoraphobia problem.) She says she would bring Jessica to her, but is unable to leave her husband because he is ill.

It's only a long walk or a short bus ride away, but Hazel hasn't been outside on her own since before Jessica was born, and feels sick at the thought of doing so. However, she loves Jessica with all her heart and can't bear to think of her being frightened or left with strangers. She phones her partner, Rob, but he has a problem at work and says he can't help her. They argue (**Conflict situation 2**). Hazel tries to get a taxi, but the local firm is fully booked. None of her neighbours are home from work.

She gets another phone call from the neighbour and can hear Jessica screaming in the background (piling on the pressure!). In desperation, feeling sick and giddy, Hazel eases herself out of the front door and onto the driveway. She gets in the car and tries to start it. The battery has died (**Conflict situation 3**). She knows there's a bus that leaves from the end of the road in five minutes and thinks of Jessica's favourite nursery rhyme as, one step at a time, she gets to the bus stop just as the bus pulls in. She gets on it in time to see Rob following behind in his car.

### Pace and tension

Begin stories at a point of change for the characters. Get into the action quickly. Provided you have given enough information to make your reader care about the outcome, they will stay with you.

The pace of your story should vary. Raise the dramatic tension, and then slacken it off before you bring it back with a vengeance. Look at how an artist uses light and shade in a picture. If it was all the same colour, it wouldn't be as interesting to look at. The same is true of a story.

Look at how Shakespeare varies the mood and atmosphere in his plays. Even in a tragedy, there are lighter moments of humour before the tension is brought back.

Raise the tension by imposing a time limit. This works well in James Bond films and some murder mysteries, where the character has twenty-four hours to solve the problem or find the killer, and avert disastrous consequences.

Note that even in these films and stories there are lighter moments, and very often a 'love interest'.

Confined spaces also work well! It was no accident that Agatha Christie set her stories in remote country houses or on trains. Cruise liners are also a good setting – particularly if there is a reason why the people cannot leave the ship – for example, a salmonella outbreak (which hopefully doesn't affect the hero and heroine of the story!).

### Magic Points

★ Introduce problems in threes.
★ Give your characters difficult choices.
★ Don't allow situations to be solved too easily.
★ Remember to include lighter moments.
★ Conflict should be on three levels, with a balance of these throughout the story.

➤ **Exercise 1**
Make a list of possible environmental problems that could affect your characters – from a burst pipe to getting trapped in a cellar. Make a list of reasons why someone might be prevented from leaving a remote country house where they are working – for example, weather, illness, car not starting. Write about one of them.

➤➤ **Exercise 2**
Pick a character – either one of your own or one based on a picture from a magazine. What is their problem – for example, an addiction to shopping, eating too much chocolate, being unable to say 'no'? When did this start? What have they tried to do about it? What problems is this causing them?

➤➤➤ **Exercise 3**
Imagine your character having lunch with someone they dislike but need a favour from. Where do they meet? How are they dressed? What do they eat? What happens? Write the scene in full.

# Step Nine
## Believable Settings

Interesting settings sell novels! Look at the sort of books that are on offer at airports and ferry terminals. I remember several years ago Robyn Sisman's novel *Weekend in Paris* being on sale at the Eurostar terminal in London. A large number of people bought it to read on the journey.

It is easy to get carried away with your characters and what they are doing, and neglect to put in information about where they are doing it. Show the setting through the eyes and emotions of your characters. Remember that they won't all feel the same way about a place. One character may find a great sense of peace in an old-fashioned garden, whereas for another character it arouses unhappy memories. Most of my settings are based on real places, but end up as a mixture of fact and fiction. Keep a list of fictional place names in your notebook. If you are using a real place then it's a good idea to put a disclaimer at the start of your novel to say something like 'this is a work of fiction, and poetic licence has sometimes been taken with its representation of Oxford'.

I once heard of a novel set in Falmouth where the writer had created a tea-shop at a particular address that actually existed in real life. The people working in the dry cleaners (which had that address and had been there for eighty years) were pestered by callers wanting to know when the shop had changed hands. If you are going to use an address, then fictionalise the street number.

If your setting is a real place, visit it if you are able to, and gather as much information as you can. Take photographs, make sound recordings, and collect as much historical information as possible. It will all help to add depth to your knowledge of the place. Collect maps and any other information from the tourist information centre. Guided walks or ghost walks can add interesting additional information.

If you are unable to visit the place, then you can still find out enough information to write your novel. Dan Brown certainly managed to find enough information on Paris to write *The Da Vinci Code* – even if he did use a certain degree of poetic licence!

Don't get bogged down in a lot of research – or let it stop you writing the story. I once knew a lady who'd collected so much research material on post-war Poland that she couldn't remember what her initial intention had been when she started. It is best to start writing, and if you come to a bit that you're not sure about, write your best guess and put an asterisk next to it to remind you to check your facts later.

Imaginary settings are more likely to be believable if they have some foundation in truth. The locations of many of Stephen King's novels are based on the places where he used to play when he was a child. These have long since been buried under housing, but still exist in his memory and imagination.

If you are going for an imaginary or fantasy setting, think about the landscapes of your childhood. Are there places you could use or adapt?

If you can see where your characters are, then so will your reader. Visualise as much as you can – it is a good investment of your time.

Imagine you are one of your characters walking around the setting. How do they move? What do they see, hear and smell? Do they feel safe? What are the pathways like? What sound do their footsteps make? Would the time of day change anything? Are there houses, shops and other buildings, or is it a wild landscape?

Write down as much as you can about your visualisation. Look for magazine pictures that remind you of houses, landscapes and objects. Create a map for your setting. (This is particularly useful if you are writing a crime novel.)

I heard of one writer who created a 3D map of her setting using Fimo clay. She also made little models of her characters to check that what she was expecting them to do in bed was physically possible – that they didn't end up needing three hands!

Create a history for your setting. Most of the information won't be needed in the novel, but it will add depth to the story – a bit like giving your characters a childhood.

Think about folklore – real and imaginary. For instance, a writer friend of mine made up a story about a haunted telephone box for a Hallowe'en party. Within days, ten people who heard the story had reported sightings of a ghostly presence. At least one other writer has used this technique in a novel.

> **Magic Points**
>
> ★ Interesting settings sell novels.
> ★ Make sure you can visualise your settings clearly.
> ★ Look for inspiration in magazine pictures.
> ★ Raid your own life.
> ★ Create a history for your setting.

> **Exercise 1**

Visualise one of your characters in a setting. Write two paragraphs from their viewpoint – one in which they like the place and the other in which they don't. This gives you the beginning and ending of a short story. You can begin with the 'don't like' version and end with the 'do like' – with whatever was the catalyst for change in the middle.

>> **Exercise 2**

Write about a house or other building that forms part of your setting. Imagine you are taking someone on a guided tour of it.

>>> **Exercise 3**

Go to a café you've never been to before. Jot down 'glimpses' or brief notes about it – for example, 'smell of apple-wood smoke', 'bacon frying and cinnamon toast', 'sparkle of frost on pavements'. See if you can create a poem, or the first paragraph of a story.

# Step Ten
## Sensory Detail

Colours, sounds, smells and textures help to bring your writing to life on the page. Adding sensory detail gives your reader a complete picture of characters and settings.

Think of it as adding brush strokes for detail. For instance, if a story is set on a beach, the scene will come to life if you describe the sun sparkling like a mirror on the blue sea, the crying of gulls overhead and the shrieking of children as they run in and out of the waves, the feel of hot sand on bare feet, the smell of suntan lotion, and the taste of salt and vinegar on chips.

Imagine this
Which of the following examples gives a clearer picture?

*Version 1*
Kate and Louise met for coffee in a small café a week before Christmas.

*Version 2*
Kate and Louise sat on unmatched wooden chairs at the window table of The Copper Kettle. Kate had short, dark hair. Louise was wearing a pink velvet hat. They were drinking big cups of frothy coffee and eating meringues bursting with fresh cream and plump raspberries. Outside, the pavement sparkled with December frost.

Is there a scene in your novel that could be given a sensory makeover? Remember that no two characters will see the scene in the same way. The smell of vinegar might remind one character of moonlit strolls with a boyfriend sharing a cone of chips, whereas it might remind another character of the hours she spent cleaning windows for a disapproving aunt.

If flowers and butterflies feature in your story, make sure they appear at the right time of year. If you're not sure you've got things right, check with an expert. There will be someone in your local wildlife group who will be able to help you.

Remember that details like the seasons, the weather and the clothes your characters are wearing need to change. Make sure that your characters aren't walking around in a t-shirt and flip-flops in the depths of winter when there is snow on the ground – unless they are a little eccentric!

Think about how various types of weather make you feel. Jot down ideas in your notebook. You may find these useful. Do you feel agitated when the weather is stormy and a strong wind is blowing, threatening to flatten your fence? Are you frightened of thunderstorms?

Take time to notice the blue shadows of a deep snowfall and the glitter of frost on the pavements, or the way your toes and fingers tingle with cold. Think about the feel of electricity in the air when a storm is brewing, and the sultry heat of a summer day. Use these elements to add mood and atmosphere to your story.

Write some poems – it's a good exercise for creating interesting, and brief, descriptions.

Writing can be a bit like the fashion industry when models do photo-shoots wearing winter coats in the summer, or bikinis in the depths of winter.

If you decide to send some short stories to magazines, then you will be sending Christmas stories in the summer, or beach stories in the winter.

Start to see every experience you have – good and bad – as a creative opportunity. Instead of getting upset when your garden is damaged by high winds, or your car won't start because of the cold weather, write about the experience instead, and see how many ways you can use the situation creatively.

Don't forget to use birthdays, anniversaries and Christmas in your writing! These can be useful for raising dramatic tension – particularly if opposing characters are forced to be together as a result of environmental factors like bad weather.

Notice how evocative smells can be. What smells do you associate with your childhood? Could you use these in your novel?

What textures do you like and dislike? I had one friend who hated the feel of cotton wool, and another who couldn't bear to touch raw meat. This caused unbelievable stress for her when she fell in love with a man who was addicted to steak and chips!

Check through the work you have done so far on your novel, and make sure you have appealed to all the physical senses. Visualise each scene, taking note of what your characters can see, hear, feel, smell and taste. Remember that they will react differently to these experiences.

What sort of music do your characters listen to? Try listening to some as you write, and see if this generates some new ideas.

---

**Magic Points**

★ Sensory detail brings your writing to life.
★ Check environmental facts.
★ Use your notebook.
★ Make sure your characters react differently.
★ Don't forget special occasions.

---

> **Exercise 1**

Pick one smell from the following list and write about it for five minutes without stopping:

★ washing powder
★ lavender
★ coffee
★ bleach
★ onions

* toast
* roses
* mint
* polish
* apples.

Does the smell hold a memory for you? Is this something you could use in your novel?

## ▶▶ Exercise 2

Describe the texture of one of the following materials:

* cotton wool
* velvet
* glass
* silk
* sandpaper.

Do the same with a colour, and write for five minutes.

## ▶▶▶ Exercise 3

Borrow some music that you would never usually listen to from a friend. Listen for a few minutes with your eyes closed. What can you see? Has this given you inspiration for a story twist, or a new character?

# Step Eleven
## Keep Writing`

Set yourself achievable daily, weekly or monthly goals so that you work steadily towards a completed first draft. Keep reminding yourself that you are working on a first draft – and expect that it will be messy. Novelist Anna Jacobs refers to this as 'the dirty draft'. Allow your ideas to change – you are aiming for completion, not perfection.

If you are not achieving the goals you have set yourself, then review the situation and decide on a smaller quota of words. It is better to complete a smaller amount and feel good about it than to be constantly battling against something that is difficult. Reward yourself for the effort you put in.

Treat your writing like a proper job. (Hopefully, one day it will be!) Value what you do, and keep building that picture inside your head of your ultimate goal.

Create a collage of what that success would mean to you – whether that is being able to help other people, driving a lipstick-red sports car, or buying a holiday villa in Italy. Pin the collage up where you can see it regularly. (If you think your family might laugh at you, stick it on the inside of your wardrobe door.) Focus on that dream for a few minutes every day.

Whenever you go into a bookshop or library, identify the section where your book will go when it is published, and make a space for it. Imagine it being there.

Keep looking for fresh inspiration. The writer Julia Cameron describes this as 'refilling the creative well', and recommends a weekly 'artist's date'. This could be a visit to an art gallery, a walk in the park, or a long soak in the bath surrounded by scented candles. It doesn't matter what you do, but the important thing is to do it alone so that you can truly focus.

Take a notebook with you! The object is to fill your mind with images and sensory experiences, so that your imagination has a larger pool of ideas to work from. Look for experiences that provide you with colours, sounds, smells, tastes and textures. Here are a few of my favourites:

* ★ Art gallery
* ★ Garden centre
* ★ Music concert
* ★ Walk in the countryside
* ★ Experimenting with a new recipe
* ★ Visit to a new café
* ★ Herb garden.

Hopefully you will find fresh inspiration for poems and stories, and maybe a new character for your novel. If you work on keeping your creative spark fully charged, then you will be less likely to suffer from writers' block.

If you get stuck and can't think of the next part of the story, don't worry. Novel scenes don't have to be written in order. Many murder mysteries are written with the last scene described first, and the writer works in reverse order to make sure that the clues and 'red herrings' are correctly placed. Margaret Mitchell wrote the last chapter of *Gone with the Wind* first, and then decided how the characters had ended up in that position.

Look at the way scenes in a film are shot out of sequence and arranged in the correct order later. Write a note to yourself in bold, 'new idea needed here', and move on to the part of the story that you do know. Go back later and fill in the gaps.

Ask your subconscious for help. Write the section of the story that you need help with on a piece of paper, and the time by which you would like the help, and put it under your pillow. I usually find this works for me.

Dreams can also be useful. Keep a pen and paper by your bed, and write down any interesting ones. Use them as inspiration for poems, stories and scenes in your novel. Don't forget to daydream! Stephen King calls this 'the writer's trance'.

Keep adding to what you know about characters and settings. Any surplus information can be recycled and used for other projects.

It's a good idea to keep writing short pieces and sending them off to magazines and competitions. It gets you into the habit of finishing work, working to deadlines, and submitting work correctly.

Create a 'Writing CV' for yourself. Note down any successes you have had, however small. Don't forget to include any previous writing experience you may have had as part of a job or membership of a society. For instance, if you were a member of the Womens Institute and were responsible for sending a monthly report to the local paper, this is good evidence that you have been used to working to deadlines.

Keep good records of the work sent to magazines and competitions. Include the following information:

* ★ Date
* ★ Title of work
* ★ Where sent
* ★ Closing date (if it's a competition)
* ★ Date returned
* ★ Result
* ★ Payment (you may need this for tax purposes).

Keep moving forwards with your novel. Don't be tempted to go back and change anything until you've got to the end of the story. Writing and editing involve two different parts of the brain, and if you try and do both at the same time, it's a bit like rowing a boat round in circles – you don't get anywhere. If you keep rewriting the first chapter you may never get to the end!

I find it helps to type my first drafts in bold – and I often type scenes in brief if I'm not quite sure what happens. I add more information on the second draft. This is what it looks like:

> **controlling father brought up with smell of**
> **greens and bleach in a house with no**
> **bathroom just a tin bath on Saturday night and**

**how this creates a need for wealth and**
**when he's older no matter how much he has**
**he will always feel poor and the ghost of the**
**rent man chasing him will haunt him**
**and his emotions are behind a locked door**
**in his head like the cupboard where the gas**
**meter was under the stairs.**

I found this 'writing down the page' technique in a book called *The Weekend Novelist* by Robert Ray and Brett Norris. It's particularly useful if you have a difficult or painful scene to write. Set the kitchen timer for ten minutes, and type or write as fast as you can without stopping. Reward yourself when you've finished, with coffee and special biscuits – or something stronger!

The 'rolling stone' method of writing means that your completed first draft may be fairly short – but it should contain enough plot to sustain something longer. I work through up to five circuits, adding more to scenes and developing new sections of plot and subplot. As I fill in the sections typed in bold and complete the various parts, my manuscript gradually lightens up. When it is all 'light' I know it is close to completion.

### Reminders

Make writing part of your life – a bit like cleaning your teeth. Write something every day, even if you only manage a couple of sentences. It will keep the thread of your novel clear in your head.

Don't worry about getting it right – just get it written! If you don't feel inspired to write, set the kitchen timer for five minutes and see how much paper you can fill in that time.

Play the 'what if?' game. Keep testing out the ideas in your novel. Remember to make a list of your obsessions and interests, and include some of these in the story.

Use ideas more than once! Information you gather in the process of doing research for your novel could become an article, or a letter to a magazine. Create poems and short stories from information gathered about characters and settings.

Daydream and visualise as much as you can. Carry a notebook wherever you go – and make good use of it.

> **Magic Points**
>
> ★ Get to the end of the first draft before you begin to edit or change anything.
> ★ Leave a gap if you're not sure what happens next.
> ★ Set daily, weekly or monthly goals.
> ★ Keep writing and submitting short pieces of work.
> ★ Novel scenes don't have to be written in order.

## ➤ Exercise 1

Write for five minutes about a childhood memory involving a game or a place where you used to play.

## ➤➤ Exercise 2

Write the above exercise in a different way. Think Stephen King. Play the 'what if?' game. Write in a genre you have not tried before. For instance, what if you found a doorway to the 'other world' near your den in the woods? What if you ventured into it? What if you fell asleep in the woods and when you awoke time had gone back 100 years, allowing you to solve a family mystery?

## ➤➤➤ Exercise 3

Write for five minutes about a childhood memory of either a Christmas or a summer holiday when something was said that you didn't understand. What happened? What do you remember? How did you feel?

# Step Twelve
Polishing and Submission

When you've finished your first draft, put it away for a few weeks and get on with something else. It is important that you don't lose the writing habit. Reward yourself for what you have achieved – but remember that you still have work to do.

You may need to revise your manuscript several times before it is ready to present to a publisher. Many writers get disheartened and give up at this stage. Make sure you are not one of them. Set a date for taking a second look at your manuscript. Write it in your diary, and keep to it.

Stay focused on the 'success' picture inside your head.

You may well feel tired, emotional and a bit disorientated now that you have got to the end of your story. This is normal. Take extra care of yourself for a few days, drink lots of water, and get plenty of sleep. Go out somewhere for a day or an afternoon. See what fresh inspiration comes to you.

Allow as much time as you can when you look at your manuscript again. Keep to the date you planned – bribe yourself, if necessary, to sit down and read through your work. When you do, you will probably find there are some bits that are better than expected, and other sections that are muddled and unfocused. Don't be discouraged. It can all be put right.

Print off a hard copy and read through your work – aloud, if possible. Mark any bits where more information is needed. Cut any sections that drag or don't add to the forward movement of the plot.

I find working from a hard copy better than the computer screen because it enables me to check the beginning and end of each chapter at the same time to make sure I've got a good opening sentence and that I've ended the chapter on a 'page-turner' or 'cliffhanger'. It is also easier to spot typos and repetitions.

You may need to repeat this process several times until you have a polished novel that is ready for publication.

If punctuation and spelling is not your strong point, don't rely on the spell-check on your computer. Ask a trusted friend if he/she will look at it for you. Don't expect them to do it for nothing. It is a time-consuming job.

If you are in a real muddle, you may decide to have a professional critique done of your work. However, this can be expensive, so shop around for the best option. Be prepared not to like what you hear. Also, bear in mind that the critique is only one person's opinion. If you feel passionate about your story, then so will many other people. Don't give up on it! Keep going until you get the result you are looking for.

Pay attention to positive criticism. If someone tells you your characters or settings are weak, and suggests ways to improve this, then take note and see if you can incorporate some of the changes.

Keep forming contacts with other writers – or anyone else who supports your writing ambitions. These are a great help on days when you do feel despondent. Don't show your work to anyone unless you feel happy to do so.

Work hard on polishing your first few pages in particular. This may be all the space you have to impress a publisher or agent. The first sentence or paragraph is known as the 'narrative hook', and should pull your reader into the story.

Put as much effort into your last page as you have into the first one. The last page of your novel will build your readership for your next novel.

If you feel that the ending of your novel could be stronger, brainstorm for thirty minutes and see if you can come up with ten possible endings. The ending of the novel should mirror the beginning in some way – or answer a question posed at the start of the story.

List ten possible last lines. Choose the three most promising ones. Then map out the last scene of the book that will leave your reader waiting eagerly for the next one.

### Submitting your novel .

It is a good idea to complete your novel before you start sending out sample chapters and your synopsis. The reason for this is that your ideas may change considerably by the time you finish the book. Think of the stress you'd be under if a publisher or agent wanted the finished book, and you'd only completed the first three chapters.

(This happened to one of my students. She had to invent a month's holiday in Australia and chain herself to her desk. She achieved her goal but lost nearly two stone in the process, and her husband almost left her!)

I'd even suggest having a rough idea of what your next book is about. Publishers and agents are in the business to make money. They want to know that you have a number of ideas that will hopefully make them rich too! It is quite possible that you will be asked to submit another novel within a specified time.

Decide whether you are going to target publishers or agents. Some publishers only accept submissions via an agent. Do your research. Most writers have a section at the beginning of their novel where they thank various people. Make a list of the agents mentioned by writers who publish stories that are similar to yours.

Look in the *Writers' & Artists' Yearbook* at the list of agents who accept unsolicited work. Check their websites to see if your ideas are similar to theirs. Do the same for publishers. Read articles in writing magazines, and find out all you can about the publishing industry.

Some writing conferences have free ten-minute appointments with agents and publishers. These are worth taking advantage of – especially if you have a completed novel to offer them. Check out their details before you go. They will be impressed that you have bothered to do your research.

Be confident when you meet them. They are human! Be proud of what you have achieved. They will want to know:

★ who/what the book is about
★ who you are
★ why you have written the book.

Be prepared to answer questions about your story and characters. You may be asked to fill in a publisher enquiry form. Take your time with this, and give them as much information as possible. Don't leave any boxes blank! The aim of this is to find out as much about you and your work as they can – how much writing you have done so far, what you have had published, and how determined you are to promote your own work.

This process helps them to weed out people who might be difficult to work with, or who expect to sit and sip champagne while somebody else promotes their book for them!

If you are asked what ideas you have for promoting your work, try to come up with at least three ideas. For instance, if your book involves food, maybe you could do a book signing in a local café, with free coffee and home-made biscuits for anyone attending. If your story has an artistic theme, maybe you could team up with a local artist and do a joint venture to promote their work and yours.

The days of an author writing a book and leaving it to the publisher to sell it have long gone. It is very much a shared activity now, and the more you can do to help yourself the better.

The novel you submit to a publisher should be correctly punctuated, typo-free and proof-read. Never tell them it is their job to do this! Most publishers and agents require work to be submitted in Ariel or Times New Roman 12 font. Double-space your work, and indent the first line of each paragraph and each new line of dialogue. Don't leave additional gaps between paragraphs, unless you are indicating a line break or change of scene.

Include a cover sheet giving the title of your novel, the word count, and your contact details. Remember to enclose sufficient return postage.

Some publishers and agents accept e-mail submissions – and this does save a lot of money on postage. Check the format and line spacing they require.

Make sure you send them something that looks neat and professional. Send them exactly what they are asking for.

It's a good idea to put your name and the title of your work in the footer in small type, just in case your submission falls off an editor's desk. (I'm told this happens quite often.) It will then be easy to reassemble your chapters.

Most publishers and agents want to see your first three chapters (approximately 10,000 words), a short synopsis, and a covering letter. Some may ask for a CV. Your covering letter will probably be the first example of your writing that they see, so it should strike just the right note. (See the example at the end of this chapter.)

### Synopsis

A lot of writers panic more about their synopsis than they do about writing the novel. Many call it 'the dreaded synopsis'. It is a narrative summary of your novel, and is basically a selling document for your book. Many publishers and agents only want a brief one-page synopsis, but it is best to check individual requirements and then modify your submission as necessary.

It should be written in the present tense, and the opening paragraph should hook the reader. You can include dialogue or quotes from the novel to give a flavour of the story.

Include the following information:

★   the title of the book
★   where and when it is set
★   who the main characters are – what their goals are and what is stopping them from achieving them
★   the themes explored in the novel

★ major events, and how they are resolved
★ how the novel ends.

Writing a synopsis is difficult, but it should help you to identify any weaknesses in your plot and characters.

Don't send your work in a fancy folder or spiral binding. Use a large paper clip or elastic band. Enclose a large self-addressed envelope with return postage. Some writers add a note on their submission to say that they are happy for their work to be shredded if not required, and enclose just a small envelope for a reply.

Don't expect a quick response. It can sometimes take a minimum of three months. With a novel it is reasonable to do simultaneous submissions – send it to several different places at the same time. Remember to target either agents or publishers. If an agent agrees to take you on, they are not going to be pleased if your work has already been sent to some of the publishers they may have contacted on your behalf.

If you are sending work to women's magazines or competitions, send it to one place at a time.

Don't be discouraged by rejection. Keep going. Get as much work out there as possible. Remember that fashions change – in publishing, as in everything else. What was unpublishable a few years ago may well be eagerly accepted now.

If you have written something that doesn't conform to what most publishers appear to want – or if it is something that you don't wish to compromise on – you may decide to self-publish your work. The end result is the same – you will still have to do a lot of work in order to promote and sell it.

**NOTE** – Self pubishing is very different from 'vanity publishing', where you can part with a lot of money for a small quantity of a low-quality product. With self-publishing, you are in the driving seat! You can set yourself up as a publisher and buy a block of ISBN numbers (the number that goes on the back of the book and makes it traceable in bookstores) from Nielsen Book Data.

When you are happy with your manuscript, go in search of a printer who will do the work you want doing at a price you are happy to pay. Visit several printers, get lots of quotes, and don't say 'yes' until you feel happy with your decision. Ask to see samples of the work they have done, and don't be afraid to ask as many questions as you need to.

### Magic Points

★ Finish your novel before you submit it.
★ Check publishers' individual requirements.
★ Be prepared to promote your work – have some ideas ready.
★ Don't be discouraged by rejection.
★ Think about self-publishing.

> **Exercise 1**

Have you got the best possible title for your novel? Brainstorm for ten minutes and see how many possible titles you can create. Aim for something memorable that sums up the essence of your book.

>> **Exercise 2**

Visit a bookshop and look at ten back-page blurbs. How many of these would you feel inspired to start reading – and why? Can you include these elements in your synopsis?

>>> **Exercise 3**

Write a short biography for yourself. Think of ten ways you could promote your novel when it is published. (You may be asked by your publisher or agent to think of at least three!)

Example of agent/publisher letter

Author's Name
Address
Date

Mary Jones
The Agency
3 Bath Road
London
W6 7LA

Dear Mary Jones

I enclose the first three chapters and synopsis of a 90,000-word romantic suspense novel, *The Silent Lover*, for your consideration.

I have set the story in northern Cyprus, an area I know very well. Great care has been taken in my research to ensure that I have been accurate in details concerning the police and any related institutions. However, any police procedural material is merely background to the harrowing and tension-filled story of my heroine, Lucy Marlow.

I feel my novel would appeal to female readers of the contemporary novel who enjoy the works of J. D. Robb and my favourite author of yours, Penny Evans.

I completed my MA in writing at Bath University last year, and this is my first completed novel. I have a second story mapped out, which is also a romantic suspense novel, as I would like to carve a name for myself in this genre. I have been a teacher for 30 years, and have written sections for English GCSE textbooks.

I look forward to hearing from you.

Yours sincerely,
Name

## Sample synopsis

Grace Andrews
20 Church Street
Leominster
Herefordshire
HE28 1SR
Tel: 01432 45678
e-mail: grace@hotmail.co.uk
www.grace-andrews.co.uk

## Synopsis

*The Butterfly Ball* is an 85,000-word contemporary romance with a touch of magic, set in the village of Hestercombe in rural Gloucestershire. Readers of Joanne Harris and Christina Jones would enjoy this book.

Eleanor Richards has just been made redundant and is on the point of being evicted from the cottage she rents by Todd Eliot, her handsome but arrogant landlord, because he objects to her plan to start a New Age therapy centre.

Eleanor's taste in clothes is viewed as eccentric by the locals and she has overheard Todd telling the vicar that he'll do his best to make sure she moves on. This makes Eleanor even more determined to continue with her plans. She confronts Todd in the community orchard, and discovers there is a softer side to him.

Eleanor is surprised to find an ally in Agnes, the elderly woman who runs the local bakery, who has a lot to say about Todd, his family and the legend attached to Ashby Court, their rambling historic mansion.

Eleanor is even more surprised to receive an invitation from Todd to the annual Butterfly Ball. She attends the ball but leaves early. On getting home, she finds that someone has tried to set fire to her cottage. She suspects Todd was responsible, but cannot prove it.

Todd comes to visit her the following day and proposes a modern-day marriage of convenience. Eleanor refuses, but shortly afterwards everything with her new business starts to go wrong, and she is falsely accused of dishonesty.

As Eleanor starts the slow process of clearing her name, she discovers the truth about what happened on the night of the ball. She and Todd fall in love, and plan to marry at the following year's Butterfly Ball.

# Epilogue

Getting your book published is not the end of the story. Most publishers will expect you to do your fair share of marketing and selling it. (This is where all that social networking comes in!)

Good luck – and keep writing.

Remember to stay focused on the reasons why you are writing – the people and organisations who are likely to benefit from your book, either by the knowledge you have given or the money you have raised.

Help other writers who are following you along the same pathway.

Be generous, and that generosity will be returned to you – with interest.

# Appendices

Appendix 1: Books for Writers

*Becoming a Writer* by Dorothea Brande,
pub. Penguin. Putnam  ISBN: 0-87477-164-1

*The Artist's Way* by Julia Cameron,
pub. Pan. ISBN: 0-330-34358-0

*The Vein of Gold* by Julia Cameron,
pub. Pan.  ISBN: 0-330-35285-7

*Write it Down, Make it Happen* by Henriette Anne Klauser,
pub. Simon & Schuster. ISBN: 0-743-20938-9

*Indestructible Self-belief* by Fiona Harrold,
pub. Piatkus. ISBN: 0-7499-2495-0

*Writing Down the Bones* by Natalie Goldberg,
pub. Shambhala. ISBN: 1-57062-424-0

*A Writer's Space* by Eric Maisel,
pub. Adams Media. ISBN: 978-59869-460-4

*The Weekend Novelist* by Robert J. Ray and Bret Norris,
pub. A & C Black. ISBN: 0-7136-7143-2

*On Writing* by Stephen King,
pub. New English Library. ISBN: 0-340-82046-2

*'The Writer's Toolkit' booklets* by Sue Johnson,
pub. Greenwood Press.

## Appendix 2: Magazines for Writers

### *Writers' News/Writing Magazine*
Warners Group Publications plc, 31–32 Park Row, Leeds LS1 5JD
Tel: 0113 200 2929, www.writers-online.co.uk

### *Writers' Forum*
Select Publisher Services Ltd, PO Box 6337, Bournemouth BH1 9EH
Tel: 01202 568848, www.writersforum.com

### *Mslexia*
PO Box 656, Newcastle-upon-Tyne NE99 1PZ
Tel: 0191 233 3860, www.mslexia.co.uk

### *Leaf Writers' Magazine*
Leaf Books, 2 Hastings Place, Penarth, Vale of Glamorgan CF64 2TD
www.leafbooks.co.uk; e-mail: contact@leafbooks.co.uk

### *The New Writer*
PO Box 60, Cranbrook, Kent TN17 2ZR
www.thenewwriter.com

### *Facts & Fiction*
42 Mill Street, Belper, Derbyshire DE56 1DT
www.factsandfiction.co.uk

## Appendix 3: Websites for Writers

### Arvon Foundation
60 Farringdon Road, London EC1R 3GA
www.arvonfoundation.org

**National Association of Writers' Groups**
PO Box 9891, Market Harborough LE16 0FU
e-mail: secretary@nawg.co.uk; www.nawg.co.uk

**Romantic Novelists' Association**
www.romanticnovelistsassociation.org

**Society of Authors**
84 Drayton Gardens, London SW10 9SB
Tel: 0207 373 6642; www.societyofauthors.org

**Nielsen Book Data UK**
BookData Editorial,
89–95 Queensway, Stevenage, Hertfordshire SG1 1EA
Tel: +44 (0)845 450 0016; www.isbn.nielsenbook.co.uk

**BBC Writersroom**
1st Floor Grafton House, 379–381 Euston Road, London NW1 3AU
e-mail: writersroom@bbc.co.uk; www.bbc.co.uk/writersroom

**Arts Council England**
14 Great Peter Street, London SW1P 3NQ
Tel: 0845 300 6200; www.artscouncil.org.uk

**Writers' Guild of Great Britain**
40 Rosebery Avenue, London EC1R 4RX
e-mail: writersguild@aptsolutions.co.uk; www.writersguild.org.uk

**The Writer's Toolkit**
www.writers-toolkit.co.uk